THE GREAT INDIAN VASTU HANDBOOK: A SCIENTIFIC MANUAL FOR HAPPY, PEACEFUL AND PROSPEROUS LIVING

DR. RAMCHANDRA NATH SHARMA

To all my readers

Contents

Foreword

Man is the best creation of nature. From animals, plants, insects, aquatic animals to humans, no one is above the laws of nature. While other creatures have been moving in almost the same way for centuries under the laws of nature, humans are not standing still. With the help of advanced and developed brain, man has conquered the world without going against the laws of nature. Not only have they created societies and civilizations - they have conquered disease, they have sent rockets to different planets to unravel the mysteries of the universe. All obey the laws of nature No one could change it Not even people Man has only understood those laws of nature and put them to use Man is so advanced, yet he is helpless to the greater natural forces Wherever animals surrender helplessly, in the case of storms, floods, earthquakes, tsunamis, droughts, droughts, fires, etc., human beings are also trying to find a way out of them through the application of science. In this way people are constantly moving forward The goal of building this human civilization is to make life easier and more beautiful. Vsat keeps life easier and simple. It is the ancient hindu science and technology that if applied properly can create a happy, prosperous and healthy and peaceful living.

Preface

As a consultant and researcher of this ancient science of vast for many years, I naturally hoped to write a guidebook that will help the general readers. The aim of this book is specifically that. I shall be highly pleased if it helps to create a harmonic and peaceful living for mankind and my readers.

Acknowledgements

To those great sages and practitioners who created this great science.

Prologue

Vsatu science

Man is the best creation of nature. From animals, plants, insects, aquatic animals to humans, no one is above the laws of nature. While other creatures have been moving in almost the same way for centuries under the laws of nature, humans are not standing still. With the help of advanced and developed brain, man has conquered the world without going against the laws of nature. Not only have they created societies and civilizations - they have conquered disease, they have sent rockets to different planets to unravel the mysteries of the universe. All obey the laws of nature No one could change it Not even people Man has only understood those laws of nature and put them to use Man is so advanced, yet he is helpless to the greater natural forces Wherever animals surrender helplessly, in the case of storms, floods, earthquakes, tsunamis, droughts, droughts, fires, etc., human beings are also trying to find a way out of them through the application of science. In this way people are constantly moving forward The goal of building this human civilization is to make life easier and more beautiful For this We want his suitable residence in the city or in the village And this habitat should be done in such a way and in such a land that it can save us from danger, from the wrath of nature and help us to develop our life. There is a scripture on which side the front of the house will be, on which side there will be doors and windows, there will be kitchen etc. and that is vastu.

Our Home and Vastu

Vsatu protects us

The science of the construction industry can be called Vastu. Or it can be said that the energy that is created by the combination of different objects in the construction industry is the ecosystem. Good or bad energy is emitted depending on how or where things are kept in the home or office. Ecology is an art by which the balance between good and bad energy can be maintained. In addition to the construction of the building, the soil test where it is located, the way the road goes in front, the direction the building faces, the water system, the surrounding environment are all included in the ecology. vastu is also mentioned in our ancient literature and scriptures. According to Raj Vallabh, an ancient vastu expert, not only a good house but also a good life requires compliance with the ecosystem, that is vastu. For him, the things that he has asked to emphasize are - 1. According to the city in which the building will be built, its usefulness. Direction 3. Soil 4. Day 5. The judgment of the constellations according to the position of the eco-man has roughly five main points in a building. - Place, air, water, fire and soil. Peace, prosperity and good health will be maintained among the people if coordination between these five is maintained. In vastu it is said that Brahma created our body for the abode of the soul. Just as there is a balance between water, air, etc., so there is a need for balance between the five basic elements for our body to live. The ecosystems of the ancient sages who wrote this vastu are scientific. They say that every ecosystem has energy and that this energy creates the ecosystem which they have termed as inert energy and living energy. Now look, what did Einstein, the greatest scientist of all time, say? He has proved that the universe, which is made up of the mass and energy of matter, is mutable. That is, mass can be converted into energy and energy into mass. Our ancient sages have also said that every human being has an aura of aura which is most often seen on the body of a great man especially around his head. Which they have termed as 'Divya Kanti Balay' The same is true of gods and goddesses. It's not a fantasy or a cannabis story, but was discovered in 1939 by Russian scientist Simon Kirlian. He noticed that when he was pointing his fingers at the photographic plate in the case of a high voltage electric field, a kind of energy was emanating from it and the discovery of aura energy from the body. Scientist Kirlian also invented instruments to measure that energy What he proved with the help of modern science, but thousands of years ago our Vedic sages realized without the help of any scientific instrument that they have given the name of life force and inert energy. Otherwise, without any instrument of the truth-seeking Indian sages, this discovery would have been contained in the leaves of the Vedas - no one would have known.

CHAPTER TWO

Our home is our life

There are two types of energy: Negative Energy or Positive Energy and Positive Energy In the case of the ecosystem, real estate must be selected and housing must be considered so that the negative energy does not work - only the positive energy will work. When negative energy works, it will lead to various physical and mental ailments, violence, mental disorder, unrest, loss, loss of wealth, etc. Whether we build homes, offices, factories, warehouses, shops, there is an overall energy two energy that we cannot see with the naked eye. Modern Energy Scanning Device Help us build all these so that they are filled with positive energy and if we stay there for a long time we can be filled with positive energy so that our life can be happy. It is also important to keep in mind that the negative energy generated due to physical faults can be positively reduced by various means - various colors, reflectors, power ceiling devices, essential oils, symbols, etc. - without breaking the house. Ecology, factory land or garden house - whatever you go for, there are three things to look for. Number one is the cosmic force that is affecting your chosen or electable land The reason why Rahukala, Barbela or Shubhakala, Mahendrakshan or Churamani Yoga etc. are mentioned in our ancient scriptures and calendars is due to the fact that during Rahukala or Barbela evil energy or Negative Energy tends to be generated in large quantities. Number two is the presence of various substances, metals, animal skeletons, etc. in the lower part of the earth or in the womb, which tends to produce negative energy which has a bad effect on the houses, factories or anything else built on the earth. And number three is the collective energy that the house built on the ground generates that spreads over the people living in that house. Therefore, houses, factories, gardens, shops, shops, etc. should be built in such an angular position on the land in such a way that it will generate negative energy, it will be a reservoir of positive energy. In our ancient scriptures again, when it comes to land selection, 'Kurmaprastha land is given a high place based on all scientific reasons. The omnipresent cosmic energy or energy is stated in our Vedas and the main Upanishads, this cosmic energy is controlling every activity of this infinite galaxy, all living or non-living matter from every atom in the universe. It is called 'Brahman' in the scriptures This energy is energizing and controlling the planets - stars, space, constellations, space, constellations or galaxies. It is also known as the vital force, again, somewhere chi, ki, mana argon. The Bhopal Gas Accident proves that the people of the house where 'Agnihotra' is performed regularly and regularly 'Agnihotra' for the welfare of the people are endowed with positive energy. The poisonous gas did no harm to the occupants of the house where it was practiced, while the occupants died in other houses. Scientific experiments can be used to prove the positive effects of positive energy at different levels. This positive energy is abundant in beaches, waterfalls and religious places It is believed that this energy is abundant in the Tibetan monastery area on the Indo-Tibetan border and that the people there live up to 260 years. In one part of Greece, Arunachal Pradesh and Totalakonda in Visakhapatnam, the people of Babikonda live up to 100 years because of this positive energy radiation. Cement and Steel Produce Negative Strength Cement and steel are recognized all over the world as an essential component of modern housing. Negative energy emitting steel and radon gas emitting cement cannot be ruled out. But if we can energize them while preparing them, then they will not generate negative energy after being used in the house, they will radiate the above positive energy. Moreover, the quality and strength of these components will increase Cell Phones. When it comes to energy, we need to talk about those cell phones that are very much in use nowadays and are essential nowadays because they emit very radioactive and radioactive radiation. This energy is negative For a long time, scientists did not want to acknowledge its harmful consequences But after European scientists proved it, it became universally accepted And they have also set a safe level Its effect is more damaging to the eyes and the ability to produce children This radioactivity works like the rules of a microwave oven When a cell phone works and is in direct contact with the body, it can be very deadly because it emits 5,000 to 16,000 units of negative energy. As a result of continuous use, any special organ of the body gets damaged If not used again after a while it stops radiating negative energy and returns to normal So it should not be kept in the chest pocket or hand It can then damage our heart and since the different parts of the palm of our hand are directly connected to different limbs, it can damage other limbs if used continuously for long periods of time. Eco-oriented East, West, North and South. These four aspects have a special effect on the ecosystem. It is important to have knowledge about this when constructing a building. Earlier, the direction was calculated by looking at the shadow of the sun. Now, with the help of advanced technology like magnetic compass, the direction is determined accurately. Although there are four main aspects in general, there are a total of ten aspects in Bastu. However, there are eight directions in the compass. The compass can rotate up to 180 degrees in total. There are 45 degrees for each direction. It is necessary to check the degree level for each direction. North, South, East, West - In addition to these four main directions, there are four more subdivisions. These are always angular. These are - northeast angle or northeast angle, southeast angle or fire angle southwest angle or southwest angle Angle Northwest Angle or Wind Angle The ninth aspect is the sky and the tenth aspect is the abyss. The north side of Bastum is considered extremely auspicious. The ruler of this side is Kubera, the god of wealth according to Hindus. That is why the northern side is identified as the direction of financial and professional development. Mercury is the northernmost planet. The chest and abdomen of the ecosystem are on the north side.

Therefore, it is important to keep the north side of the house open, bright and beautiful at all times. According to modern ecologists, the North Pole emits large amounts of good energy from the north. This energy is necessary for all members of the household. Therefore, ecologists are advising to keep the north side open so that the positive energy of the North Pole can enter the house well. The south-south side is always marked as the worst side in the environment. But that is not always true. It can be said that the bank of all good energy in the north is the south. It is better that the south side is not very open. The Hindu deity Yam is the ruler of this side in Bastu. So if the south side of the house is more open, the members of the house will be afflicted with various ailments and even death. Members of the open house on the south side can also get involved in lawsuits. Money and prestige will increase if there is a closed wall on the south side. The representative planet in this direction is Mars. East - very strong direction. The lord of this planet is Devaraja Indra. Indra is the god of rain, prestige, festivities and energy. As well as the representative planet to the east is the sun, which in itself is a huge source of energy. The effect of the sun is to improve life. So we identify the east as the direction of progress. It is important to keep the east side of the house open, bright and clean. On this side, if there are only closed walls instead of doors and windows, improvement in life will be hindered. Having a bathroom on the east side of the house is a big obstacle in the bathroom. Remember, obstacles in the east mean obstacles in your life as well. West - This is the direction of establishment and prosperity in life. The lord of this side is Vishnu, the god of rain, fame and fortune. The representative planet in this direction is

Saturn. It is not advisable to keep the west side of the house very open. East energy i.e. energy emitted from the sun is stored towards the west. As the sun rises, the source of energy shifts from east to west as it descends from east to west. It is better not to have the main door of the house on the west side. This destroys the possibility of earning money. North East - Very good direction in Bastum. The ruler of this side is Shiva, the best god of Hindus. Its representative planet is Jupiter. Donates wealth, prestige and good health. Northeast is a very auspicious place for students. Strong magnetic energy is emitted from this direction. Building a toilet on the northeast side of the house can kill the whole family. Combustible substances should not be placed on this side. It is better not to do big construction. Southeast - If you have a grumpy, sensitive well-wisher, this southeast is a lot like him. The lord of the southeast is Agnidev. Its representative planet is Venus. When the sun comes to the southeast, its mood is extremely fierce. This is the time when the sun is at its most extreme. This fierce form is likened to fire. It is better to do fire work in this direction. It is important to be careful when storing and building things in this direction. Southwest - This side is ruled by a monster named Niriti. Its representative planet is Rahu. This is the strongest aspect of the house as the magnetic energy emitted from the northeast is stored in this direction. Proper use of this aspect can lead to a very strong and healthy life. This aspect is identified as the aspect of wealth, health and confidence. If used in accordance with the environment, the southwest side will bring fame. But misuse will bring many problems. Money will run out. Depression, anxiety and even suicidal tendencies can occur. Misuse of the Southwest in the workplace is a cause of inattention to work by employees.

Northwest - This side is dominated by wind. Its representative planet is the moon. This aspect is very unstable as it is the main component of wind. Proper use of this aspect brings many opportunities in life. Professional life can be improved. However, its misuse in Bastum causes confusion. It can also lead to illness. The Ecological Significance of the Different 'Aspects' of the Land on which a house is to be built If there are a total of ten aspects arranged north-south-east-west, then the role of eight aspects is very important in ecology. These eight directions are: east, west, north, south, northeast, fire, southwest and wind. The first four of these are called the main 'directions' The last four are called auxiliary 'no' According to Indian scriptures, each of these eight aspects has a deity or Dikpala I Here 'deity' means 'power' According to ecology, different types of energy are constantly radiating from these four directions and four angles and affecting the earth in various ways. Therefore, for the sake of human perfection, prosperity and welfare, while maintaining balance with all these forces of nature, various etiquettes, customs and prohibitions of life have been described in detail in Ecology. The purpose of this article is to present all these complex instructions and provisions of ecology in simple language to the general public. So that the reader can lead his life in a healthy and simple and peaceful way, one after another writings and discussions on ecology have been published continuously. However, this time we will look at the importance of the eight aspects It is discussed in detail below: (1) The deity of the north is the deity of this direction - Kubera Soma or Chandra. Significance indicates allied location to the north That is why the northern side of the ecosystem should not be confined (2) The southern deity is the presiding deity of this direction The importance of this aspect is enriching Happiness in life is conducive to the development of peace and spirits (3) The eastern deities are Indra and Surya According to the scriptures of importance, this aspect is the ancestral place It is necessary to keep the east side of the land open while constructing houses for permanent residence If this aspect is restricted, there is a risk of harm to the health of the householder (4) The western deity is the presiding deity of the western side Varuna 6 Significance depends on the size of the householder's reputation, value, and reputation (5) Ishan Kona Adhikarta is the deity of this corner Som Shiva The importance of this angle breeder 6 So this aspect should be kept as flawless as possible (6) Southwest angle deity is the deity of this angle southwest. Significance depends on the size of the household and the responsibilities of the householder. (6) Agni Kon Adhidevata Agni is the presiding deity of this angle. Significance This angle affects the provision of healthy, vigorous, wholesome health (6) Vayu kone adhidebata Vayu kone adhidebata-marut 7 Significance This angle provides the householder's public relations In other words, this angle influences the householder's relationship with the majority This relationship can be both good and bad The good effect of the wind angle is the gain of ally 6 Adverse effects increase the likelihood of enemy increase and various losses In this way the above eight aspects have a profound effect on the quality of life Properly applied to Vastu, these effects can contribute to happiness, prosperity and prosperity in human life.

Some useful vastu practical instruction of land and house

Vastu science

Land (1) Square land is best. The size of the land should be square or rectangular. However, the ratio of length and width of armpit land should not be more or less than 2: 1. (2) Oddly shaped land should always be avoided. For example, hemispherical arms, hexagonal shape, hexagonal, pentagonal, oval, circular, triangular, arc-shaped, hemispherical, semicircular, pointed, directional land is not good for the ears. (3) The history of the land should be known. Such as whether the land was a graveyard of any animal or human. Homes should not be built on such land. (4) The soil of the land should be examined. Land with surgery should not be bought. And the electric wire should not go over the land at high power. (5) The north east side of the land should be open. It is better to have a reservoir in the northeast. On the southwest side of the land it is better to have tall trees, big houses, hills or mounds. (6) It is best to have a road around the house. The road on all three sides is also good. However, it is better to have roads at least on both sides. If there is a road on one side of the land then it is better if it is on the north or east side. Not good on the other hand. The house should never be built on a 'T' or 'Y' shaped junction. Corner land (6) Land at the junction of two roads is attractive. But before buying such land, one thing has to be kept in mind, according to the rules, if you want to build a corner land, you have to leave the corner of the corner land. This angle should not be to the north-east or south-east or south-west. Building a house (6) It is better to do land worship, foundation stone, boundary wall and house owner according to the horoscope at auspicious time. The boundary wall must first be built before the house can be built. The south and west walls must be raised and raised between the walls around the boundary wall. Main Entrance (9) The main entrance of the house depends on which side of the land there is a road. The entrance to the house can go in any of the four main directions. However, the north or east facing main entrance is better. (10) The main entrance of the house, when sitting on either side of the north, south, east or west, divide each side into equal 9 parts, leaving 3 parts from the left and place the main entrance in the fourth part. (11) If the road is not actually north, south, east or west, then the entrance of the house may be placed in this way. Window (12) The window of the house should be placed at the top. The windows of the house should be placed in such a way that 'cross ventilation' or horizontal light-ventilation is provided. (13) According to ecology suitable place to place windows - (a) east (b) north (c) north-east east (d) north-east (e) north-west north (f) north-west (g) south Direction. The position of the stairs (14) is made on the south or west side of the land and the fruit is good. The stairs will rotate clockwise upwards due to normal clockwise rotation. (15) If it is not possible to make stairs to the south or west, stairs should be made to the south-east and north-west. The northeast side of the land should be light and the north-east side should not be stepped. As you climb the stairs, you will climb from east to west. Elevator (18) The ideal place to place a multi-storey house is in the south, west or south-west area. Kitchen (18) is a volcanic area on the south-east side of the house. That's why the kitchen should be on the south-east side. If for some reason it is not possible to have a kitchen on the south-east side, the kitchen can be done on the north-west side of the house. (17) The kitchen should not be in the north-east, south-west or Brahmasthala of the house under any circumstances. When cooking, it is advisable to keep the face of the housewife facing east. (19) The kitchen platform should be facing east. It is better to keep the gas cylinder under the platform. Of utensils The cupboard should be placed on the south or southwest side. (20) The kitchen faucet should be in the north east corner. The water mesh or filter is also on the north-east side. The pantry will be on the northwest side of the kitchen. Toilets (21) Toilets will be located on west, south, north-west side. The toilet commode or pan should be placed along the north-south. Bathing (22) It is best to take a bath in the east. If not possible, it can be done in the west and north-west. Tube well (23) It is best to make a tube well on the north-east side of the house. However, if it is not possible, it is better to go to the north-west. Tube wells should not be installed in the south-west or south-east. Septic tanks and soakpits (24) are best placed in the west corner of the house and in the mid-north under the ground. Alternatives can be made underground in the Middle East and East. Overhead Tank (26) The overhead tank will be on the south-west side of the house. The outhouse (26) should be built on the north or west side without touching the boundary wall. The height of the outhouse should be less than the height of the main walls. Power Connection (26) It is best to connect the house to the south-east. Alternatively, never connect electricity to the south or north. Because the north-eastern side is the ecological place according to the ecology according to the panchabhautika theory. That is why electricity connection or indeed fire connection, is not classically favorable. Porch (29) The porch of the house should be on the north or east side. The level of the roof of the veranda and the roof of the house should not be the same. Garage (30) The garage of the house should be in the south-east or north-west area of the house. Terrace (31) Terrace should be built in the northeastern part. Living Room (32) The living room of the people and guests of the house will be on the east or north-west side. The master of the house will entertain the guest facing east or north. Reading Room (33) The reading room should be on the north or west side of the house. You should look east or north while reading. The lid of the reading table should be green. It is auspicious for the door of the reading room to be on the north-east side. Thakur Ghar (34) Thakur Ghar should be built on the north-east side of the house. This aspect is the place of Jupiter according to astrology. According to scientists, this aspect is filled with an abundance of positive energy. If it is not possible to have a Tagore house on the north-east side in the owned flats, then a small Tagore house can be built in those flats in Brahmasthan. If it is not possible, the seat of Thakur will run on the north-east side of any house. Kartar's bedroom (35) Kartar's bedroom will be on the south-west side. The master's bed should be at least three inches away from the south-west wall. While sleeping, the head of the master should be on the south and the feet on the north. The head should never be in the north. (36) The door of the bedroom should be placed on the north east side. (36) The main cupboard should be placed on the side of the bed on the south-west side of the house, so that the cupboard has a face on the north side. If it is not possible to keep a heavy cupboard in the south-west, money will be kept in a small cupboard north of the house. Mezzanine floor (36) If you want to make mezzanine floor in the house, it can be done on the south side of the house. Basement (39) Basement should be done on the north-east side of the house. However, the basement should not be south or west of the house. Brahmasthan (40) Brahmasthan is in the middle of the land. There should be no beams, columns, pillars, walls. For similar reasons, it is undesirable to place a heavy object in the middle of a room. If it is possible to separate the clown house (41), it is best to do it on the north-west side of the house. Boxroom (42) Small items of the house, old furniture, bedding, old utensils can be kept in the south-west side of the house or in the elevated place or loft on the south-west side of any house (except the north-east). Garden (43) It is best to plant on the north-west side of the house. Alternatively, north-east gardening should be done. Generator (44) The generator house of a multi-storey flat is best done in the south-east. Alternatives should be made in the north-west. But by no means do I want to convey that I recommend for the mother to be inactive. Furniture (45) The ideal place to keep the mirror is the east or north wall. No large mirrors can be hung on the south-west or south wall. (48) The wall clock should be hung in any direction except south. But it is best to hang on the east side. The southwest corner of the south wall of the southwest room of the house is the best place to hang pictures of late ancestors. Alternatively, it should be hung on the wall of any house on the south-west side. (48) Large refrigerators can be placed on the south-east or south side of any room. Smaller refrigerators should be placed on the northwest or west side. (48) However, no refrigerator, large or small, should be placed on any northeast wall. (49) It is best to place the TV in the north-west of any house. Since the TV is an entertainment device, the alternative should be to the south-east. (50) Large sofas should be placed on the south-west, south or west wall of the sitting room. (51) Washing should be done by keeping the washing machine in the east room. Domesticated animals (52) Cows and goats can be kept outside the house in the north-west of the land. Dogs and cats will be on the north-west side of the stairs or in a cool place. (53) Small birds, fancy birds can be kept in the north-west of the house or house. Colorful fish should be kept on the verandah or on the north east side of the house. Drawing room or sitting room (54) The living room can be made to the east or north-west of the house. Dining room or dining room (55) can be made east or west of the house. Living Room (56) Living room mainly depends on the main door. This is because the room in front of the main door is usually used as a living room. The east or west house can be used as living. The place to keep musical instruments (56) for various furniture of the house.

CHAPTER FOUR

Musical instruments

Specific places to keep musical instruments like are also indicated in the Vastu. Professional artists should place various musical instruments such as guitar, harmonium, sitar, sarod, sarangi, tanpura, veena, bean, tabla, modern synthesizer, piano etc. in the north-west corner of the north-west corner of the house. The musician planet Moon. And in the north-west corner, according to astrology, the place of the moon is said to be auspicious for the musician if musical instruments are placed there. The artist's musical life will be full. However, the large-sized piano of the old days should be kept in the south-west corner of the north-west side of the house. Miscellaneous shoe storage (56) Shoe storage space can be provided on the south or south east wall of the house to the south and west of the house. Alternatively the north-west house can be placed south or south-east. In no case should it be placed on the north-east of any house. Arbajana (59) Never store Arbajana in the house. As soon as the dirt accumulates, take it out with a broom. Garbage can be placed on the south side of the house, alternatively on the northwest side. The land facing the boundary wall (60) should be done on the north-eastern side. West-facing land should be done to the north-west. (71) North facing land- North east to north side. South-facing land - to be done on the south-east side.

CHAPTER FIVE

Any work is interrupted? Follow these tips

Surya namaskar

Anyone can worship the sun god. However, remember that the sun god is worshiped very early in the morning. Therefore, whenever you want to recite Surya Purana or chant any mantra, do it only in the morning. If your work gets lost in time, there is nothing to worry about. Or if the work is not done at all, then understand that your sun is weak. If anyone is going to fight these problems, he needs to strengthen his solar system. However, some special measures need to be taken on Sunday. Let's find out. This solution also works well So there is no need for any special day to please Suryadev. But since Sunday is the day of the sun god, there are many benefits to worshiping him on this day. So every Sunday, if you don't have rice, some red chillies and red flowers, put roli in a copper pot. Then offer offerings to Suryadev with this water. Worship the sun god with these mantras

Salutation to sun

Read Suryapurana on Sunday. With 'Om Surya Namah', 'Om Hrim Hrim Surya Namah', 'Om Ghrini: Suryadiom' and 'Om Haran Hrim Harunas: Surya: Namah', anyone can worship the Sun God. However, remember that the sun god is worshiped very early in the morning. Therefore, whenever you want to recite Surya Purana or chant any mantra, do it only in the morning. These remedies are useful to please the sun god If you want to strengthen your sun, you should donate copper pots, red cloth, wheat, molasses and red sandalwood as much as possible on Sunday. Also, remember to never give water to the sun god without bathing. Take special care of this on Sunday Oil and salt should not be eaten on Sundays when the sun is weak. Because Suryadev gets angry when he plays with salt. Also, food should be taken at once. Iron and wood should not be traded. One should also refrain from criticizing anyone. Also, don't lie.

CHAPTER SIX

Tulsa tree

It is very bad to dry the Tulsi tree, keep the Tulsi fresh in this way Drying the basil tree can bring bad luck in life. If you do not want the basil plant to dry out, it is important to choose the right soil. Most people who believe in Hinduism plant Tulsi trees in their homes. At the same time water is given in it every day and worship is done. A green basil tree at home is considered a symbol of prosperity. This is why people take special care of the basil plant. But even after regular care, the basil tree dries up. Drying the basil tree is not considered auspicious. The dried basil tree is considered a symbol of bad luck. It is said that mother Lakshmi got angry when the basil tree dried up. It is said that if care is taken and care is taken when planting basil, it can be protected from drying out. Let's know the important rules regarding Tulsi. Soil for the basil plant According to religious beliefs, drying the basil tree can lead to bad luck in life. If you do not want the basil plant to dry out, it is important to choose the right soil. It is said that red or sandy soil is best for basil. In this way the basil tree will remain green Dung manure is used to keep the basil plant alive. Wet dung should not be given to the tree. Dry the dung and grind it and apply it on the basil tree. This will keep the basil green. Basil leaves should not be broken from the tree on this day In some homes, people break basil leaves without taking a bath, which is not considered proper. It is said that a basil tree should never be broken without taking a bath. Also, basil should not be broken on Ekadashi and New Moon days. On the eleventh day, offering Tulsi to God is broken on the previous day. Remember to water the basil It is believed that the basil tree should be watered with raw milk on Thursday. It is said that it keeps the moisture in the basil for a long time. Also makes him always look green. According to religious beliefs, water should not be given in Tulsi on Sunday. Tulsi should not be watered during the rainy season. Because it threatens its roots. Keep clean It has been said that when the buds begin to come on the basil tree, then it must be understood that the burden on the tree is increasing. In such a case, the basil buds should be broken. Also, it should be offered at the feet of Lord Vishnu on any Thursday. It is believed that doing so brings blessings of Lord Vishnu.

CHAPTER SEVEN

Rambha Apsra

Virgin girls can observe Rambha Tithi, Apsara Puja Mantra According to the mythology, Apsara Ramva originated from the churning of the sea when the gods and demons were churning the sea. Later she became an apsara of heaven and lived there. To bring good luck in life, you must observe Rambha Tithi. Rambha Tithi is celebrated every year on the third day of Shuklapaksh in the month of Jyastha. Many call this day Rambha Tij. It is believed that fasting on this day enhances both beauty and good fortune. It is believed that it is very good for women to celebrate this special day.

Rambha

Origin of Ramva: According to the mythology, Apsara Ramva originated from the churning of the sea when the gods and demons were churning the sea. Later she became an apsara of heaven and lived there. So if any worship is done in the name of Apsara, then it brings benefits in life. According to astrology, the rules of observing Rambha Tithi You can bathe in any river at the beginning of this special day. Then you can sit facing east with a clean cloth and praise the sun. You must light a lamp for the sun. On this day, married women must worship Goddess Lakshmi and Goddess Satimata with full rituals. Then as good fortune comes, so will beauty. Because Apsara Ramva is considered as a symbol of beauty. Lakshmi must light a lamp during worship.

Rambha

Mantra of Rambhapujo Om Divya Namah Om Bagishchaya Namah Om beauty priya namah Om yauvan priyaya namah Om Arogya Kamna Namah Om pranipriya namah om urjascalaya namah Om Devapriya Namah Om Aishwarya Pradayaya Namah Om Dhandai Dhanda Rambhaya Namah Importance in Rambha : It is believed that on the third day, a person attains happiness, prosperity, good fortune and beauty in the middle of this pujo and ministerial utterance. Also on the one hand married women can keep this fast for the longevity of their husbands. Unmarried women can keep this vow to get the husband of their choice.

CHAPTER EIGHT

Many have differing views on the afterlife However, according to those who have studied the soul or evil forces, there is another life after death Many people believe this power and many people think it is wrong Easily find out if there is an evil force in the house According to those who have studied spirits or evil spirits, there is another life after death. Many people have misunderstood this idea and there are many who have realized this miraculous power in their own consciousness. Many have differing views on the afterlife. However, according to those who have studied this subject, the presence of all these energies is present in us. However, it is easy to know if you have the presence of this evil energy in your home. There are special rules to know about this. Take one third of sea salt in a clear glass. Fill the rest of the glass with vinegar. However, it should be taken in such a way that salt and vinegar do not mix in any way. And care must be taken so that no handprint of the glass falls. Place this glass in the presence of sunlight in a place in the house where it will not be easily pushed or touched. But the whole thing depends on faith. Many do not believe in the presence of evil spirits. If after 24 hours you see that the vinegar in the glass is clear and does not change, then it must be understood that there is no negative energy in the house. And if you see that the color of the vinegar changes, then it must be understood that there is the presence of evil energy in the house

CHAPTER NINE

This zodiac sign is always blessed by Lakshmi, the goddess of wealth. They make a lot of money and live in luxury. Know that the people born in this lucky sign are always rich. In astrology, many special things have been said about the nature and future of all the signs of the 12 signs. Find out which zodiac sign natives are very lucky in terms of money and money. This zodiac sign is always blessed by Lakshmi, the goddess of wealth. They make a lot of money and live in luxury. Know that the people born in this lucky sign are always rich. People born under this sign are very rich Taurus - According to astrology, those born in Taurus are blessed by Goddess Lakshmi. There is never a lack of money in their life. They make a lot of money from their hard work. They succeed in everything. They get high status in life and create different identities.

These people became very wealthy after the age of 30. Cancer: Mother Lakshmi's grace is always on the people born in Cancer. These people are intelligent and make good money from their talents. People born under this sign enjoy all the comforts of their life. With hard work, you will achieve great success in your career. They take great care of every happiness of their family. Leo: People born in Leo are very good leaders. Besides the sun god, Goddess Lakshmi also blesses them. They make their place with their talent, hard work and at the same time earn a lot of money. These people take expensive hobbies and spend a lot for their livelihood. Even then, they never run out of money. Rather they own many assets. Scorpio: Mother Lakshmi is always kind to those born in Scorpio. Surprisingly, they do not even have to work hard to earn money. They easily get luxurious life and bank balance. These people are very smart and luck is on their side..

The second sign of the zodiac is Taurus. The ruling planet of this sign is Venus. People of this zodiac sign are usually of beautiful priestly and artistic nature. It can easily win the hearts of the opposite sex. Boys and girls of this zodiac sign are attracted to more than one person. According to the scriptures, there are four signs with which they have sexual pleasure. People of this zodiac sign have affection, tenderness, love in their minds. They are always steadfast in their goals. Their friend luck is quite good. Their nature attracts everyone. Find out who they enjoy sex with. Taurus has a lot in common with Scorpio. According to astrology, Taurus boys and girls are happy with this zodiac sign. They can understand each other better. It affects the sex life. When Taurus and Scorpio are related, both of them get happiness in sexual life. Taurus boys and girls are also happy with their relationship with Cancer. In fact, they both deal with their confidence as they choose to embark on their play activities. Can satisfy each other's sexual needs. Good friendship is also formed between these two zodiac signs. As a result of physical union, the relationship between these two signs becomes stronger. Taurus is also happy with Virgo. Taurus and Virgo have a lot in common. Virgo boys and girls, look for someone who is faithful and honest. On the other hand, this is the characteristic of Taurus boys and girls. That is why there is a great similarity between these two signs. They are happier in physical union with each other. Cotton is also ruled by Venus. That is why there are many similarities between the people born in Tula Rashi and Taurus. Both of them became very romantic. That's why these two have a lot in common. The boys and girls of Taurus are also satisfied with sex with Tula Rashi. The bond between the two is strong. If a person is born in English from 21st April to 20th May or in Bengal from 7th Baishakh to 8th Jaishtha, he is born in Taurus. Taurus is the second sign of the zodiac. According to astrology, those who have this zodiac sign have more affection, tenderness, affection than other zodiac signs. This personality is quite interesting. According to astrology, the auspicious color of Taurus is white. Good day is Venus, good number is 48. The auspicious side of this sign is the southeast corner. According to the scriptures, white coral is the auspicious gem of this sign. So if your zodiac sign is Taurus, then if you want to get sexual happiness, you will be happy with Scorpio, Cancer, Cotton or Virgo. According to the scriptures, people born in Taurus are happy in marriage just as they get sexual satisfaction with Cancer. The marital life of Taurus and Cancer is the happiest. They can spend time together. Likes with each other. Taurus is similar in nature and mentality to Cancer. According to the scriptures, all kinds of happy relationships are achieved with the right amount. It is possible to get an idea about the sexual life of a person just as one can get an idea about the character of a person by looking at the zodiac sign. An important part of life is physical intercourse.

Who will be associated with which zodiac sign at this time, is described in astrology. According to the scriptures, there are four signs with which Taurus boys and girls have sexual happiness. People of this zodiac sign have affection, tenderness, love in their minds. They are always steadfast in their goals. Not everyone agrees with them. Happiness does not match. They are happy to meet only these four signs. The scriptures describe the personality of a person in terms of characteristics. So before getting involved in a relationship with someone, find out what the boy or girl of that sign is like. Will there be any happiness with him or not. So find out which four zodiac signs get sexual happiness in Taurus boys and girls.

Life can be changed with just a few eco-tips. Many people ask, is it possible to change the destiny in vastu? The answer is of course possible. But for him some rules have to be obeyed. These 15 eco-friendly tips will change your life! Rule-1: If there is a blank wall at the entrance of the house, put a picture without leaving it empty. Rule-2: Mind restless? Then sit a little to the north-east. Better a poor horse than no horse at all. Rule-3: Put a picture on the north-east wall where a long way can be seen, you can also put a picture of sunflower. Rule-4: You can put a family picture to improve the family relationship. But of course to the southwest. It is better if the picture is framed in gold. Rule-5: Place the reading table on the east side. Rule-6: You can put a picture of sunrise on the east wall. Social relationships will be better. Rule 6: Try to make the sum of the doors and windows of the house an even number. Rule-6: Always put a picture of a red horse to keep the money supply good. Rule-9: While sleeping at night, the wife lies on her husband's left side and maintains marital peace. Rule-10: Keep the bottom of the bed clean and empty. Good for the future. Rule 11: Keep gas and water faucets in the kitchen as far away as possible. Rule-12: Bedroom spell houses on the southwest side of the house. Rule-13: Keep the fish aquarium on the northeast side, life will improve. Rule 14: Place a green tree on the east side of the house. Relationships between family members will be better. Rule-15: Practice following the above 14 rules.

CHAPTER TWELVE

vastu, where to build a house, how to use the things kept in the house, these are explained in detail. On the other hand, the rules of bathing in the environment have also been mentioned. It is often seen that people bathe to keep the body clean but also make the bathroom dirty. Ecologically, these habits are considered to be very faulty. Let's find out what kind of mistakes you make while bathing, which should not be done. Clean the bathroom and go out. Never leave the bathroom dirty during bathing. When you go out to bathe, make sure that the bathroom is clean. It is believed that keeping the bathroom dirty means making Rahu-Ketu angry. Which has a negative effect on people. Don't leave wet clothes in the bathroom, don't forget to leave wet clothes whenever you take a bath. Because in reality it is considered a big fault. Wash wet clothes and match on the roof or veranda. Wash dirty clothes before bathing Always wash dirty clothes before bathing. Do not wash dirty clothes after bathing. Do not leave it after washing, let it dry immediately. Discard laundry water Dispose of dirty water after washing. Try to keep the bucket filled with clean water. Don't keep your hair in the bathroom Some people have a habit of leaving their hair in the bathroom after bathing. According to Bastu, this is very wrong. If you leave your hair in the bathroom after bathing, Shanidev and Mangaldev get angry and give bad results.

The work done also deteriorates. Not only this, with the help of fire you can do welding and you have to work hard for it. Turn off the faucet After bathing, turn off the faucet properly as running water creates ecological defects. This not only wastes water, but also damages resources and honor. Do not keep the remaining water in the bucket. People come out of the bathroom after bathing, leaving the remaining water in the bucket. Don't do it at all. Fill the bucket with clean water. Do not keep empty buckets in the bathroom. Fill the bucket with water after bathing. If not filled, keep the bucket upside down. Do not leave water containers empty Depending on the ecosystem, keeping water containers empty encourages financial crisis. Also, be careful not to scatter things in the bathroom, but keep them neat and tidy. Vastu tips to bring good luck to your home If you are thinking of buying a new home or moving to a new home, there are several eco-tips that you should keep in mind. vastu recommends proper layout, shape, and direction so that all ecological elements are consistent. Ecologists recommend that you follow the ecological tips for prosperity in your new home. What is Vastu? Vastu is an ancient Indian science that outlines guidelines for the design of buildings and temples and is widely followed in different parts of India. It considers factors that affect a site, among other factors such as terrain, roads, surroundings, sun exposure, the earth's magnetic field, orientation and other elements of nature.Vastu considers houses as living souls and tries to achieve positive energy by mixing the five elements of earth, fire, water, space and air. It is the energy of the home that affects the mental health of all its occupants.

When it comes to ecology, location and orientation are important and property selection is the first step. Ecology says that whichever direction the face of a house is - east, west, north or south - it is a good choice, because there are advantages in every direction. The location of a family kitchen, its beating heart, directly affects the health and resources of the occupants, while the design of the bedroom directly affects health, career and personal life. The location of the house of worship has a significant effect on the wealth and peace of the household. The placement of furniture can affect the energy balance of a house, which in turn can have a good or bad effect on one's physical and mental well-being. Health and well-being can be improved by placing mirrors in strategic positions throughout the home.

Vastu-tips for the entrance Vastu Tips to Bring Happiness to Your Home The entrance to a home is an entrance through which all energy flows in and out. As a result, it should be located in a favorable direction. According to the main door ecology, it is best if the door faces east, north or northeast when leaving the house for the betterment of fortune and wealth. A footwear rack, trash can or water-based decorative items should not be placed in front of the main entrance as they will impede good energy flow in your room. If you build an entrance, make sure it is made of high quality wood and is large enough. To create a pleasant energy flow, make sure the front door is well lit and decorate it with an ornate nameplate. Choose bright colors that will attract good energy. Also, avoid putting antiques or animal faces on the door as they bring bad luck and dullness.

Vastu-tips for the living room Vastu Tips to Bring Happiness into Your Home The living room serves as a hub for family and social gatherings. To keep the living area clean from clutter, it can feel big. As for the living room, its orientation should be towards north, northeast, east or west. Living rooms are often furnished with couches, chairs, dining tables, televisions and other electrical devices. Ecology recommends that heavy furniture should be placed southwest or west of the living room, while electronic gadgets should be placed south-east. It is important to make sure that your living room is properly arranged and that all its corners are brightly lit, as it acts as a powerful source of energy. The living area can be made more harmonious by using a combination of color and earthy colors. According to ecology, any mirror in the living room should face north. Shine your seating area with a large crystal chandelier, as it attracts good energy and richness.

Vastu-tips for the kitchen Ecology Tips to Bring Happiness to Your Home We all know that our well-being is greatly affected by what we eat and drink. It makes the kitchen an important area of any home and your kitchen design will inspire. Kitchen windows should face north, northeast or east to absorb positive vibrations. Apply bright colors in the kitchen to create a more positive atmosphere. Eco-friendly kitchen guidelines state that kitchen appliances, such as gas burners, should be placed in the south-eastern part of the room. A harmonious relationship between water and fire, the two most important elements of the kitchen, is essential for good health and prosperity. Never place sinks or washbasins next to cooking utensils, such as gas stoves or microwaves, as they have the opposite properties of fire and water. The kitchen is a major source of energy, since it contains both raw and cooked foods. Always keep food items and refrigerators in the southwest corner of your home.

Vastu-tips for the house of worship According to Vastu, worship rooms should be built from the ground level to maximize space. According to vastu, northeast, east or north faces are more favorable than other directions for the direction of the temple in the house. , Because such spaces often accumulate negative energy. Cool colors like light blue, white and pastel yellow can be used to decorate the house of worship. Avoid dark colors. Consider adding a window to the north-east corner. Enable natural light to enter the room. vastu-tips for the bedroom vastu Tips To Bring Happiness To Your Home Formula: Ecology Tips play an important role in transforming your bedroom into a peaceful haven. To ensure a strong link between health, wealth and partnership, Ecology recommends that your bedroom face south-west instead of north-east or south-east. Depending on the architecture of the bedroom, it should not be under any kitchen or bathroom as it may contribute to illness. The decor of your bedroom has a significant effect on your mood. Dark or black paint can exacerbate the tension of the relationship, it is better to go with neutral or earthy color when decorating your bedroom. If there is a workstation in the bedroom, it should be placed in such a way that the person sitting is facing east, north or northeast. Bastu suggests using a desk that is either rectangular or square. Make sure the home office in your bedroom has good ventilation, clutter free and adequate natural light.

vastu tips for kids room Ecology Tips To Bring Happiness To Your Home Formula: A child's bedroom should be a place of care, growth and development. Following the principles of ecology, this place should express feelings of love, warmth, joy and contentment as much as possible. Avoid making beds in front of mirrors or windows. The mirror drains the good energy of a room and distracts the mind, which can be detrimental to a child's ability. Sleep, focus and rest in peace. It is best to discard any unused stationery (pens that do not have refills) as they draw bad vibes. For a clear road to success, the study table or desk should not be cluttered. Do not allow your child to put shoes or slippers under the table as it may distract you from your work. Wooden shelves for bookshelves, not metal, should always be used in the north-east corner of the room. vastu-tips for the porch vastu Tips To Bring Happiness To Your Home Formula: The uniqueness of balconies cannot be overstated. You can start your day with a mug of tea and fresh air here. When looking for a new home, some people find the porch a necessity. In addition, it allows you to create a unique space in your home. A balcony facing north, east or northeast should be the preferred location for one in the house, as it receives the most sun. The porch on the south or west side should not be made. According to ecologists, heavy furniture, such as armchairs, bin bags, benches and tables, should be placed in the southwest corner of the porch. If you prefer to use a cradle, place it facing north or south. According to the principles of ecology. Mirrors in the right place at home can increase your wealth The mirror teaches us to recognize ourselves, to love. The need for mirrors in our daily life is immense. Almost all of us stand in front of the mirror once before leaving the house or returning home. There is no second option in the mirror to show yourself fit and fine starting from cosmetics. Ecology also has examples of mirror bajimat performance. According to vastu, mirrors play a very important role in transmitting positive energy in the house. Even mirrors can multiply the arrival of wealth and happiness in the house. It is important to put the mirror in the right direction Mirrors can easily get rid of ecological faults by removing the negative energy present in the house. However, in this case, the size of the mirror and the direction in which it is mounted, is of special importance. Therefore, emphasis has been laid on its proper use in the environment.

On the wrong side, putting the wrong size mirror can get the opposite result. Just as a mirror can do you good, if you don't keep a mirror in the house properly, it can be a disaster. Find out where and how to place the mirror. If you put a mirror in any direction, negative energy will be created If you put a mirror in any direction, negative energy will be created Ecology says you should not have mirrors on the south and southwest sides of your house. Since the mirror is the source of water, it needs to be placed in the right direction. The position of the mirror on the south or west wall reflects the energy coming from the opposite direction. Stay away from colored mirrors Never keep colored mirrors in the house, it has a bad effect. At the same time, mirrors should not be installed in the bedroom. Being a source of water, the mirror also gives prosperity.

However, it will only be effective if its direction is correct. Do not place the mirror on the south side of the wall of the house. This is a financial loss because this aspect of the jam. Many people look to the south for a way to improve their business, but ecologically it is not right. Place a mirror on this side of the house

There is a place of water in the north-east. Ishan means the place between east and north. You can put a mirror here. It is better to keep a mirror on the east or north side of the house. Also the mirror of 7/8 is very auspicious. The mirror should be placed on the east or north wall in such a way that the viewer faces east or north. Keep some things in mind Place a mirror in front of the dining table, it brings prosperity. Place a mirror on the north wall of the drawing room. Mirrors can be made square or round. But avoid awkward designs. Put a mirror inside the safe, it will increase your wealth. The north side is considered to be the side of Kubera, the god of wealth, and if the mirror is placed on the south side, the idol coming from the north side can be seen in the mirror, which is not auspicious. Never keep a mirror in the room that is too heavy, sharp or has broken edges. Also, triangular, i.e. three-cornered glass should not be used. This has a negative effect.

CHAPTER FOURTEEN

Dream happening and colour therapy in vastu

If you often see something in a dream, come to life and know the opportunities for improvement and good job Every human being in the world dreams of something in their sleep. Many times people do not understand the meaning of dreams, but according to astrology, there are many dreams that people see from which there are indications of the future. Even in the science of dreams, there are many things that have been mentioned, from which it is possible to get some idea of what is going to happen in the future. Again sometimes dreams warn about future events. These dreams can be anything good or bad. According to the dream scriptures, a person often has dreams which indicate how much progress he will get in the job. Let us know what is good to see in a dream and it indicates success in the job. Dream of promotion in the job According to the dream scriptures, if a person sees Swastika, Om, Vaishnava symbols etc. in a dream, it means that the possibility of promotion of that person is being created. Such symptoms are considered auspicious. It is better to see a white horse or a white bull in a dream. These signals indicate good news for the job. These dreams create the possibility of increments as well as promotions. Dream of a good job According to the dream scriptures, if a person dreams that he is winning a competition, then this sign also carries a very good message in life. When a person sees himself winning a competition, it means that he can get a big position or a good job. At the same time, the person concerned can get any position of his choice. Or the person may be relocated to a location of their choice. Dreams of improvement in life Dreams of improvement in life Seeing flowers bloom in a dream is a sign of good news about a job. This news can make your mind happy. Even if a saint, priest or mahatma is seen in a dream, it is believed that there is a possibility of improvement in the job. Also, if there is a sudden increase in the inclination of people towards religious activities, then it should be understood that there is going to be an improvement in life. Dream of a strong future Dream of a strong future According to the dream scriptures, if a person dreams that he is dressed like a king, then this dream indicates a beautiful and strong future life of that person. According to the dream scriptures, seeing yourself crowned in a dream or seen in the king's attire indicates some great good news in life. At the same time, this kind of dream strengthens the possibility of promotion of the person. According to Bastu, the color of a house brings good luck, you know? Almost every human being wants to build a house of his own. And in that case those who have their own house or flat have the desire to decorate their dream house as per their mind. And in that case, according to ecology, it is very important to determine exactly what color should be used in different parts of the house. According to astrology, each planet is associated with one color or another. And just like that, it is considered beneficial to use the colors of the natives. It is also thought that using the wrong color can cause problems for the person. Let's see what color should be used in some cases. Diagnosis of colors by direction Diagnosis of colors by direction According to ecology, the east side of the house should be white and the west side should be blue. The north side should be green and the south side should be red or pink. Judging by the angular field, it is better to have red or pink on the south-eastern side and green or gray on the south-western side. The north-eastern part should be painted yellow or light orange and the north-western part should be painted white and azure. Although people like to choose the color according to their choice. But it is very good to have white or light blue or green part of the entrance of the house facing east, it is never good to keep the entrance of the house black or brown. It is better to paint pink and light orange for the kitchen. The color of curtains, furniture, windows and doors also play an important role in the interior decoration of the house. Try to keep the color green or blue when dining, it proves to be very beneficial in digestion. The color of the house of worship is light yellow, light orange and white. The color of the newlyweds' house The color of the newlyweds' house According to Bastu, the color of the newlyweds' house should be light yellow or white, which reflects the mutual love between the two, the atmosphere of the house is pleasant and there is less chance of quarrel. Again, it is better for newlyweds not to keep their bed sheets white or yellow. In that case using red or pink colored bed sheets is considered auspicious for them. The color of the children's room The color of the children's room According to vastu, it is best to paint the children's room pink or cream. These colors increase children's concentration. Red or black should not be used in children's rooms at all. Yes, some parts of the furniture must be black. Children who are away from school with low intelligence should have white and red pink color in their house, it will increase concentration. The mind will also sit in the study. Yellow color increases concentration, so it is better to use this color in the room of students. Important issues related to color Important issues related to color Blue should not be painted on the east or south wall of the house. Besides, pictures of sea, river, fountain etc. should not be kept in the house. Red should be avoided on the north-west middle wall, whitewashing the roof is best. Bright red, maroon colors should not be used on the middle wall from east to north. Also, it is not advisable to put pictures of any violent animal or war in the house.

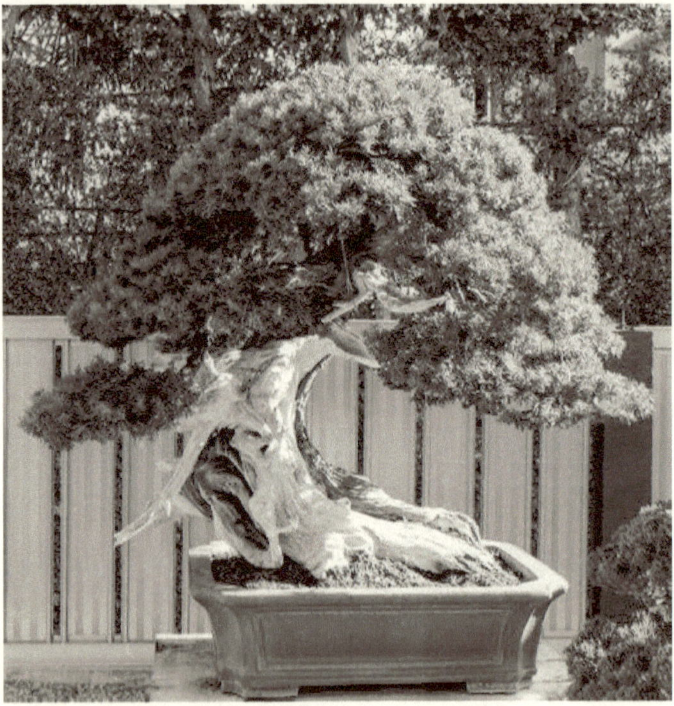

CHAPTER FIFTEEN

Bonsai

Many people plant different plants on the balcony or roof to enhance the beauty of the house. However, according to the ecology, there are some trees that bring happiness and prosperity to the family, while some of the trees in the house can be a great loss to the family. Unlucky Plants Find out today about some of the trees that will always be in danger if kept at home! Plum tree Although it is delicious to eat cool, planting this tree in the home area is considered to be very inauspicious. Lakshmi does not live in the house where cool trees are planted and there is financial crisis. The thoughts of the members of that house began to be negative. It is believed that the presence of thorns on the cool tree has a negative effect on the family. Tamarind tree Tamarind tree Having tamarind trees in the house is considered to have a negative effect. Moreover, if there is this tree in the house, many people are afraid of ghosts. Tamarind trees stand in the way of home improvement. It even affects the health of family members. Akand tree According to ecology, plants that produce milky substances should not be planted indoors. It is believed that these trees have a negative effect. Everyone in the house may be in poor health

Akand